Artists at Work

Textiles

Cheryl Jakab

Smart Apple Media

This edition first published in 2006 in the United States of America by Smart Apple Media.

Smart Apple Media
2140 Howard Drive West
North Mankato
Minnesota 56003

First published in 2006 by
MACMILLAN EDUCATION AUSTRALIA PTY LTD
627 Chapel Street, South Yarra, Australia 3141

Visit our Web site at www.macmillan.com.au

Associated companies and representatives throughout the world.

Library of Congress Cataloging-in-Publication Data

Jakab, Cheryl.
  Textiles / by Cheryl Jakab.
  p. cm.—(Artists at work)
  Includes index.
  ISBN-13: 978-1-58340-777-6
  1. Textile fabrics—Juvenile literature. I. Title.

  NK8804.2.J25 2006
  746—dc22
                                 2005057880

Edited by Sam Munday
Text and cover design by Karen Young
Page layout by Karen Young
Photo research by Jes Senbergs
Illustrations by Ann Likhovetsky

Printed in USA

Acknowledgments

The author would like to acknowledge and thank all the working artists and hobbyists who have been quoted, appear, or assisted in creating this book.

The author and the publisher are grateful to the following for permission to reproduce copyright material:

Cover photograph: Dyeing fabrics, courtesy of Rob Cruse.

Ardabil carpet made for the mosque at Ardabil, Iran, 1530s (textile), Persian School, (16th century)/Victoria & Albert Museum, London, UK/Bridgeman Art Library, p. 16 (top); Woollen figure of a jaguar, Paracas Culture, c.1500 BC (ceramic), Peruvian School/Private Collection, Boltin Picture Library/Bridgeman Art Library, p. 16 (bottom); Coo-ee Picture Library, pp. 4 (left), 12, 22; Corbis, pp. 5, 9, 10 (both), 14, 15, 17; Rob Cruse, pp. 6 (both), 21, 25; Innovative Threads, p. 24; istock, pp. 4 (top and right); Cheryl Jakab, pp. 8, 23; Leeds Tapestry, pp. 18, 19; Lonely Planet Images, pp. 11, 20; Mary Evans Picture Library, p. 13; Annemieke Mein, pp. 26, 27.

Please note

At the time of printing, the Internet addresses appearing in this book were correct. Owing to the dynamic nature of the Internet, however, we cannot guarantee that all these addresses will remain correct.

Contents

Glossary words

When a word is printed in **bold**, you can look up its meaning in the Glossary on page 31.

Textiles artists

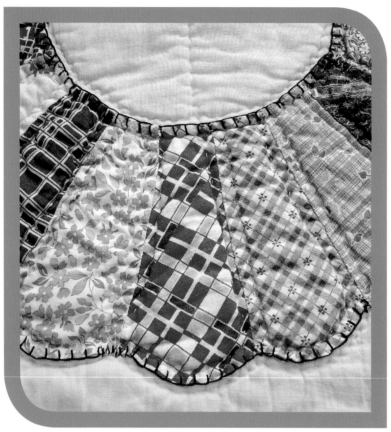

Look at these different artworks made by textile artists. Textiles artists are people who design and make artworks with fibers and fabrics. Textiles artists make fibers and fabrics into a wide variety of items including:

- ▶ decorated silk bags and shoes
- ▶ fine embroidered costumes
- ▶ colorful **patchwork** quilts
- ▶ giant patterned hooked **carpets**
- ▶ fabric sculptures

◀ This blanket is made of many different-colored fabrics.

▼ Wool is a textile that feels very soft.

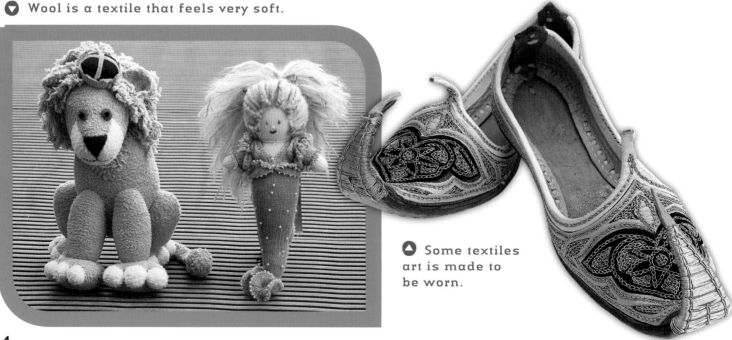

▲ Some textiles art is made to be worn.

Using textiles

All textiles artists are very skilled at creating, choosing, and using fibers and fabrics. In this book, you will find the answers to these questions and more:

- What do textiles artists need to know about fibers and fabrics to use them creatively?

- How do the chosen fibers and fabrics help the artist express their ideas?

- What is it that textiles artists like about fibers and fabrics as a **medium** for art?

- What does a textiles artist do?

"I love the richness of the textures that I can create using a wide variety of yarns, fabrics, and colors."

Margaret Tosello, textiles hobbyist

Some textiles artists work by hand, others use machines.

What are textiles?

Originally the word "textile" meant "simply woven fabric." The meaning has changed over the years, and the word is now used more generally. A textile can be any fiber, **yarn**, or other material that can be made into fabrics. It can also refer to the fabrics themselves, such as:

- threads, cords, and ropes
- braids, plaits, and laces
- embroidery
- nets and **macramé**
- woven fabric
- knitted and **crocheted** material
- **bonded** material
- **felted** or tufted yarns and threads

Woven fabrics can be made in any color or pattern.

Wool is an example of a natural fiber.

Sources of fibers

Fibers for textiles come from a variety of sources which are both natural and **synthetic**. To be suitable for textile work, fibers must be long enough to form into threads. They must also be strong enough to withstand wear and be flexible enough to be shaped. The table below shows sources of fibers that are often made into fabrics.

Natural fibers	Fiber	Source	Fabric	Characteristics and Uses
	flax	plant first used in Egypt	linen	• ancient strong and long fibers • used for knotting, weaving, and furniture
	cotton	plant first used in India	cotton	• strong fiber • used in weaving, sewing, and knotting
	wool	sheep and goats	wool	• springy fiber • avoids creasing • has a wide range of thickness and length • used in knitting, crochet, weaving, and knotting
	silk	insect cocoon	silk	• finest natural fiber • is a continuous thread but cannot be stretched • used in weaving, embroidery, and painting
Synthetic fibers	polyamide	oil or coal	nylon	• earliest commercially manufactured fiber • very strong and fine • used for stockings and nightwear
	polyester	oil	often **blended** with cotton in fabrics	• most commonly used manufactured fiber • has same uses as nylon
	elastane	complex chemical substance using oil and other chemicals	stretchy materials such as lycra	• able to expand up to 500 percent and able to return to original shape • used in clothing, especially underwear and swimwear
	microdenier	variety of fibers	fine, silky fabrics	• light, soft, and silky • thinnest of all made fibers (finer than the thinnest silk) • used in socks, nightwear, underwear, and sportswear
	lyocell	produced from wood pulp	produced under the trade name of Tencel	• soft, absorbent, and lightweight • machine washable and resists creasing • used in denim and designer clothing

Textiles work

Any method of combining fibers is described as textiles work. There are many popular handcrafts with textiles. These include knitting and crochet, **knotting** and macramé, spinning and weaving, **embroidery** and felting, fabric painting and dying. These and many other techniques are used both by hobbyists and top textile workers who create stunning art pieces.

Textiles artists are often interested in putting materials and techniques together in new ways. The artist may use the traditional processes with some **innovation** in shape, color or form. Other textiles artists develop new and imaginative ways of using fibers.

▼ Textiles artists often sell their artworks at markets.

▲ Many textiles artworks can take a long time to produce.

Creating with textiles

When creating with textiles the artist often makes a series of changes to their design. There are many choices to be made with so many fibers, colors, textures, and traditional methods available. Sometimes new ideas become popular and are copied to become new trends in fashion.

Advantages of working with textiles

Artists working with textiles describe three main advantages of their medium:

- ▶ **texture**—fibers can make artworks feel different to touch
- ▶ **color**—the artist can choose fibers of any color, or create new ones
- ▶ **variety of techniques**—these can lead to a wide variety of effects being created

"Quilting is pleasing to the touch and a challenge. Fabric and color selections are infinite, as are the rewards of this timeless craft."
Faye Scott, textiles hobbyist

▼ This wool rug is being made by hooking.

Textiles artists today

Today many textiles artists are using traditional techniques. Textiles artists are also developing new and exciting ways to express their ideas.

New fibers, old techniques

Some textiles artists make use of the new synthetic fibers and fabrics as they become available. These may be used with traditional methods to create new and surprising effects.

Hooking

Hooking is just one of the many techniques used to make carpets. Carpets are known by technique, material used, and the place of manufacture. New synthetic fibers are used to make silk-like carpets at a much lower cost than using true silk.

Macramé

Macramé (say mak-rah-may) knotting techniques can be used to create artworks that look very complicated and decorative. Many of the colorful synthetic fibers now available (such as nylon) are used in macramé work.

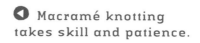

◀ Macramé knotting takes skill and patience.

Traditional fibers, new techniques

Textiles artists are also using traditional natural fibers in new ways. Traditionally natural fibers were dyed using natural plant dyes. Today, artists also work with colors produced by synthetic dyes. These are combined with natural fibers to create a rainbow of colors not possible using dyes from nature.

Computerized sewing and knitting machines allow artists to create detailed designs with traditional fibers. Creating with programmed machines is much faster than working by hand.

The Artist Speaks

"My challenge is to build up strong structures with fibers that are themselves soft and flexible."
Gabriella Falk, textiles sculptor

This brightly-colored textiles artwork is called *After Joan Miro* by Joseph Royo.

Focus on technique

Spinning and weaving

Spinning and weaving are two ancient techniques often used together in textile work. Spinning is the process of winding or rolling fibers into yarn or thread. Weaving is the process of interlacing the spun thread to form cloth. The basic processes involved are the same whether using ancient tools or modern computerized machinery.

Spinning

In spinning, short fibers are rolled together to make a long thread. This can be done with a hand spindle or a spinning wheel. The hand spindle is an ancient tool that requires skilled use. The spinner spins the spindle with one hand, while the other hand guides the fibers onto the spindle. The spinning wheel works in the same way, but the spindle is spun by a large wheel operated by hand or foot. The spinning wheel is more efficient, although it is still very hard work.

▶ Modern spinning machines can work with large amounts of fibers.

⬤ The ancient Egyptians used hand looms to create textiles artworks.

Weaving

Weaving involves **interlacing** threads in two directions, the **warp** and the **weft**. Fabric is woven on a device called a loom. Warp threads run up and down, and are secured to the loom at each end. Weft threads run from side to side. Weaving involves passing the weft threads over and under the warp threads until a fabric is woven. The effort and skill put into weaving can vary according to the intended use of the product and the value placed on it. The three main types of weave are tabby, twill, and satin weave.

Loom development

The art of weaving and loom technology was developed in China up to 4,000 years ago. Many cultures still use traditional hand looms to form fabric.

13

Textiles history

Ten thousand years ago, people took long, strong fibers from plants and animals and spun them into threads. These threads were used to create textiles. Textiles break down over time, so little has survived of the earliest textiles works.

We can learn how textiles were created from other evidence such as paintings and writings from long ago. The oldest surviving evidence of textiles work is shown in ancient carvings called Venus figurines that were made over 17,000 years ago. These female figures have what looks like knotted nets on their heads.

▼ This textiles artwork was made in the 400s or 500s A.D. and shows the Nile River.

Handcrafted textiles works were popular for thousands of years. When spinning and weaving machines were developed during the late 1700s and 1800s however, their popularity started to fall. In the 1900s synthetic fibers were developed, which meant many new fabrics could be produced very cheaply.

Great textiles traditions

There are many similarities in ancient textiles traditions, but there are also differences. These are due to the use of different materials, techniques, and knowledge affecting what could be made. For example:

- Hawaiians had no looms so they made cloth by beating bark fibers
- Ancient Chinese artists made patterned fabrics of silk using advanced loom skills
- Dyers and printers in India in the 1600s used methods for coloring cotton cloth not known anywhere else
- Europeans invented machines in the 1800s that made mass production possible
- Lacework was developed in the Europe during the 1400s and 1500s. Lacework is fine, open fabric formed by looping, plaiting, or twisting threads rather than weaving. Making lacework by hand is very time-consuming

Lacework is used for fine clothing and furnishings.

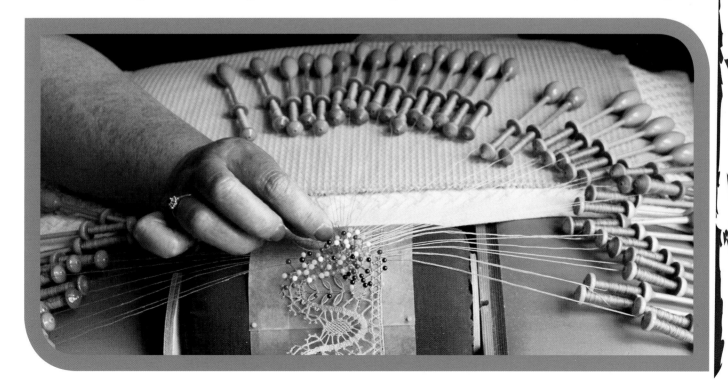

Textiles treasures

In the history of textiles artwork, a few cases stand out for their artistry. These include Persian carpet makers and Peruvian pattern fabric makers.

◀ Ardabil carpet

Date made: 1539 A.D.

Name of maker: Maqsud of Kashan

Materials used: 32,903 knots per square inch (5,100 knots per sq cm)

What it shows: Traditional elegant decorative and designs by court artists

Where it is now housed: Victoria and Albert Museum, London

◀ Woollen figure of a jaguar

Date made: around 1500 B.C.

Name of makers: Peruvian textiles artists from Paracas culture

Materials used: Wool

Where it is now housed: Private collection

🔺 By looking closely at this section of the Bayeux Tapestry you can see each stitch.

Bayeux Tapestry

One well-preserved textile treasure is a tapestry from the 1000s which now hangs in the town of Bayeux, France. It is a piece of medieval embroidery 230 feet (70 m) long, containing 1,512 figures in 79 scenes. It tells the story of events leading up to the Battle of Hastings in 1066. The scenes are embroidered in colored woollen thread on linen cloth about 1.7 feet (0.5 m) wide. The border is filled with plants, animals, and hunting scenes.

The Bayeux Tapestry has images of costume, weapons, battles, and events. It also records the appearance of Halley's Comet, which can be seen from Earth once every 76 years. The exact origins of the Bayeux Tapestry are unclear. The names of the actual workers who designed and stitched it are unknown.

CASE STUDY
The Leeds Tapestry

Textiles have always played an important part in cultures around the world. They help to provide a record of daily life, rituals, clothing, costumes, and trade through time. Many great textiles artworks are created by people getting together to make group projects. These can be giant wall hangings made by quilting, embroidery, knitting, and other means. One community textiles project is the Leeds Tapestry which shows the history of life in Leeds, England over 2,000 years. Hundreds of people in Leeds devoted their time and skills to create this story of Leeds life. It is a series of panels, with each one representing a theme such as education, health, transport, or textile and industrial heritage.

▶ This is just a small part of one of the 16 panels in the Leeds Tapestry.

○ This part of the tapestry is called "Town Hall Interior" from the panel titled "Arts for All."

The project

In 1992 Kate Russell, a textiles artist, started a project to create a textile tribute to Leeds. Leeds is a city with a long history of textile work. This includes textile factory work from the 1800s and 1900s and hand spinning and weaving from earlier times. Today, little remains of that history. The Leeds Tapestry has 16 panels, each about 7 feet by 3 feet (2 m by 1 m). From a distance, this tapestry looks like a huge abstract painting with numerous scenes of buildings, people, and places.

The Artist Speaks

"Thousands of people from across the city were involved in the research, design, and embroidery of the tapestry panels. The tapestry panels show a variety of styles, textures, and materials. It has taken tens of thousands of hours to complete."

Kate Russell, textiles artist, Leeds Tapestry project

Textiles artists work in different kinds of places depending on the work they do. Some artists may only need yarn, a pair of knitting needles, a good chair, and light. Sewers, knitters, and weavers may work with machines instead of, or as well as, working by hand. Some textiles artists' work spaces may have large tables for cutting or printing fabrics and modern computerized machinery. Designers may use computers, a dressmaker's dummy, sewing machines, and ironing presses to help create their works.

Wet areas

Felting, dying, printing, and many other textiles processes require a wet area and a place to dry finished products. This wet work needs to be kept in an area away from dry fibers and fabrics.

○ Large artworks, such as this tapestry, need to be made in big, open work spaces.

CASE STUDY
Handmade yarns

Hand spun and dyed yarns are time-consuming to produce, but for many artists the result is worth the effort. Most artists making yarns by hand use sheep or goat's wool. Some artists use a simple spindle to spin yarns but most use a spinning wheel. To make yarn on a spinning wheel, the wool must be fed into it evenly while the wheel is spun, usually by a foot treadle. The basic process is simple but there is a great deal of skill involved. The amount and thickness of the wool being fed in must be carefully controlled. Some spinners "card" their wool first, which means they fluff it up. Once spun, the yarn can be dyed using natural or synthetic dyes.

🔺 Helen Beresford finds high-quality, interesting, and unusual yarns for knitters, weavers, and other textiles artists.

Showing textiles artworks

Textiles artists show the works they make at exhibitions, competitions, markets, shops, and galleries. It is here that the public gets to admire the artist's choice of color, fiber, and technique and perhaps purchase their works. Public art galleries can purchase artworks if they think they are the best examples of the artist's work. The galleries keep and display the artwork in their public collections.

Major art shows are sometimes sponsored by companies or by artists' groups. These are an opportunity for artists to enter their works into competitions and become noticed.

Local markets are also great places to see the many and varied ways artists are working with textiles to create useful and decorative items.

◀ The texture, color, and shape of a textiles artwork can all be seen if it is put on display effectively.

Making a living as a textiles artist

Selling their artworks to galleries is one way for a textiles artist to make a living. However, few textiles artists can make a good living this way. Most artists must do other paid work to earn a living, such as teaching their art. They can also run a shop or market stall where they can sell their works to the public.

Traditional textiles workers

Traditional textiles workers around the world create highly valued textile art. They do not always get much for the sale of their works. To help these artists, organizations such as Oxfam sell these works at fair prices and return the income to the makers. This provides a fair income and helps to keep traditional arts alive.

▲ Production items take less time to create than new artwork and can be sold by the artist at markets.

The Artist Speaks

"My biggest seller is hand-spun and dyed yarn in a range of brilliant colors. I take this to a market each Saturday."
Jackie McMaster, textiles artist

Textiles artists' groups

Textiles artists, like many other people with a common interest, form groups to discuss issues of importance. There are many groups where artists can share ideas with other members who work in similar ways. Groups have been set up for textiles artists that work in particular ways. These include spinners and weavers, embroiderers, tapestry workers, felt makers, and quilters.

Online groups

Online textiles groups and associations display work, share ideas, and even sell work over the Internet. This sharing of ideas electronically has had a major effect on the medium. Many textiles techniques that had been forgotten are now available to learn about online at little or no cost.

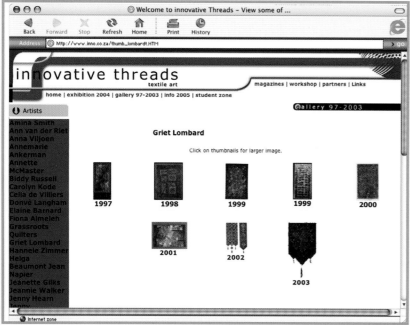

◀ Innovative Threads is a Web site that displays the textiles artwork of many artists.

Issues for textiles artists

Sharing ideas between textiles artists includes issues about health, safety, and the environmental impacts of their work.

Health and safety

Working with textiles involves using chemicals, dyes, and bleaches that may be damaging to the body. To work safely, textiles artists need to know about the substances they use and how to handle them with care.

Environmental impacts

Textiles artists need to be aware of the impact their work could have on the environment. Choice of materials, such as natural fibers or synthetics and disposal of chemicals are both issues that textiles artists consider when working. By discussing these issues with each other, textiles artists can learn ways to minimize the impact of their work on themselves and the environment.

▲ Dyes can create strong colors, but they can also be harmful if you do not use them correctly.

The Artist Speaks

"I choose to make use of recycled fabrics in my artworks. Even unwanted plastic can be recycled into useful and decorative items using ragwork."
Lizzie Reakes, ragwork artist

25

CASE STUDY
Annemieke Mein

Annemieke Mein is an award-winning textiles artist. She makes textiles sculptures using a range of techniques including embroidery, weaving, **appliqué**, knitting, sewing, and painting. She uses a variety of materials such as silk, wool, fur, cotton, and synthetics, all chosen for their color, texture, and appeal. She makes detailed larger-than-life animal and plant sculptures, wall works, and items that can be worn. Through this art she is raising awareness of the environment and the importance of looking after nature.

▶ Annemieke Mein's
Pink Emperor Gum Moth II.

◀ Artist profile

Annemieke Mein was born in Holland and moved to Australia in 1951. She enjoyed school, where she was encouraged to express her creative ideas and produced artworks in many different styles. In 1971 Annemieke moved to Victoria, Australia. Around that time, her textile artworks increased in popularity.

For each of her works, Annemieke carries out detailed research, goes on field studies, and collects examples of the shape she wants to make.

Annemieke's detailed plant and animal drawings are often bought by museums. She is known throughout the world as a textiles artist who has explored new techniques. She often combines weaving, knitting, crochet, appliqué, and other methods into one single piece of artwork.

"I especially enjoy depicting species that are not normally considered interesting, let alone beautiful, and visually enhancing their individual charms and attributes by giving a great deal of attention to their fine details."

Annemieke Mein, textiles artist

PROJECT
Make a piece of felt

Feltmaking is an ancient textile technique. Felt fabric is formed when wool fibers are pressed together tightly without weaving or twining. You simply put unspun wool in warm soapy water and press and rub so the fibers tighten into a new textile material.

What you need:

- ▶ pieces of unspun wool scraps, in various colors and types
- ▶ warm soapy water
- ▶ a brush

What to do:

1. Roll the scraps of wool together to form balls.

28

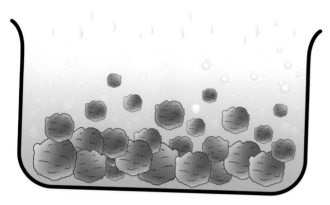

2. Put the wool balls into warm soapy water.

3. Remove the wool balls from the water and leave to dry.

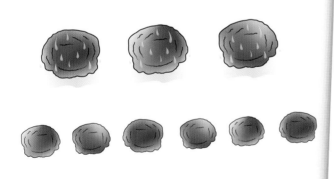

4. When the wool has dried, it will have shrunk.

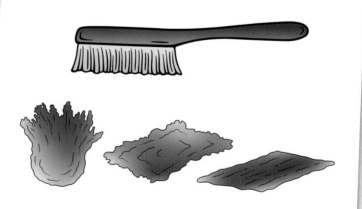

5. Brush the dry surface of the balls to change it from wool to felt.

Textiles timeline

B.C.

20 000	Bone needles used for sewing in France
15 000	Knotted headdresses used on stone sculptures
12 000	Basketwork begins in the Middle East
7000	Spindle used to hand spin fibers
5000+	Flax used to make cloth called linen by weaving
5000	Spinning wheel invented in India
4000–3000	Cloth sails are used in Egypt
3000+	Cotton used for its fiber
3000	Wool used for the first time
2800	Hemp rope produced in China
1725	Silk culture develops in China
400	Earliest known knotted carpet made
200	Use of hemp adopted in Europe

A.D.

1300s	Spinning wheel reaches Europe
1589	Knitting machine invented by William Lee in England
1785	Power loom invented for cotton weaving
1820	Crochet lace introduced into Ireland
1823	Waterproof material created by Charles Macintosh to make waterproof coats
1829	Sewing machine invented by a tailor in France; foam rubber invented
1856	First synthetic dye (aniline) created
1893	Zip fastener invented
1910	The first man-made fiber (rayon) came into production
1939	Commercial production of nylon begins
1950s	Carpets and rugs are made on low-cost, high-speed tufting machines

Glossary

appliqué work made by cutting out from one piece and applying to another

blended type of fabric produced by combination of fibers

bonded non-woven fabric made without first being made into yarn

carpets thick fabrics, traditionally woollen (but often now synthetic), commonly used as a floor covering

crocheted fabric created by using a single strand for hooking

embroidery design produced on cloth by needlework

felted dense fabric with a matted appearance

innovation new or different method

interlacing crossing two threads as if weaving them together

knotting tying knots in yarn to form an artwork

macramé art of decorative knotting

medium material used

patchwork made of patches of materials sewn together

synthetic produced from chemicals, not from natural fiber

warp in weaving, the yarn that runs the length of the fabric

weft in weaving, the yarn that runs the width of the fabric

yarn single strand of fibers spun together

Index